Much Madness

*A Survivor's Guide to Extreme States
and Self-Advocacy for Young Adults*

Edited by Calvin Rey Moen and Kaz DeWolfe

Much Madness: A Survivor's Guide to Extreme States and Self-Advocacy for Young Adults / ed. Calvin Rey Moen and Kaz DeWolfe

First Edition, September 2019
ISBN: 978-0-578-58381-5
LCCN: 2019915075

The Hive Mutual Support Network
PO Box 1021, Brattleboro, VT 05301
www.hivemutualsupport.org
bratthive@gmail.com

A digital version of this guide is available at
www.hivemutualsupport.org/MuchMadness.

Cover, illustrations, and interior design by Kaz DeWolfe

Contents

Introduction 5

Children Don't Belong in Cages......................... 13
    Jolie Mahan

Brain Blender 23
    Anonymous

From "Notes on the Unfathomable"..................35
    The Borderline Academic

Finding Community 47
    Kaz DeWolfe

Within the Fields of Possibilities 57
    Jodi Girouard

Nightmares and Demons and Death? You're
    Fine...63
    Calvin Rey Moen

Trying to Do the Right Things...........................73
    Malaika Puffer

Much Madness Is Divinest Sense.......................83
    Jess Stohlmann-Rainey

An Incomplete Resource Guide 93

Acknowledgements and Attributions

The editors would like to thank members of the Hive Mutual Support Network who read submissions and helped select essays for publication.

This book was published with a grant from the Vermont Department of Mental Health from a portion of its Mental Health Block Grant set aside for an Early Episode Psychosis Initiative.

Excerpt from "So Many Ways to Be Beautiful" by Jacks McNamara reprinted from *Inbetweenland* (Deviant Type Press, 2013).

"If I can stop one heart from breaking" by Emily Dickinson reprinted from *The Complete Poems of Emily Dickinson* (Little, Brown, and Company, 1924).

Excerpt from "'Hope' is the thing with feathers" by Emily Dickinson reprinted from *The Poems of Emily Dickinson Edited by R. W. Franklin* (Harvard University Press, 1999).

"Much Madness is divinest Sense" by Emily Dickinson reprinted from *The Poems of Emily Dickinson: Variorum Edition* (Harvard University Press, 1998).

Introduction

This isn't the kind of guide that gives step-by-step instructions. No one else can tell you how to survive. All we can do is make space for sharing stories. We can talk about how we survived, with the hope that it will spark survival strategies in someone else. It may be through telling our stories and hearing others' that we achieve survival.

That doesn't mean this book isn't instructive. Even from this very small collection of personal stories, themes and patterns emerge. These themes might inform radical change if we connect the dots and form conclusions.

Overcoming isolation

Our authors described learning to hide their differences. We sometimes call this "passing as sane," or "masking." In some of these stories, masking resulted in isolation, when the authors had no one to talk to about their pain. Other times, masking resulted in liberation, when they successfully escaped harmful situations. In her essay, Jess Stohlmann-Rainey writes, "Passing is a privilege not all of us mad people are able to achieve, especially if we are otherwise marginalized. It is also a privilege that reinforces the abuses of the mental health system and creates the expectation that mad people should assimilate." However, in her case, she found that it was the only way she knew to escape institutionalization.

Some of these stories are about seeking out supportive communities and relationships. A few of our contributors describe a need for safety to talk about extreme states. They identify peer relationships as one resource. Some contributors found spiritual or activism communities where they could connect with others.

Jolie Mahan writes about being in and out of institutions where other patients were their greatest source of emotional support. These places had rules prohibiting patients from contacting each other outside of the program, but Jolie and their friends from the hospital broke the rules and stayed in touch. "It ended up being one of the wisest choices we ever made because, as we soon found out, the struggles of living with mental illness don't end in the hospital. They were only just beginning," writes Jolie.

In her essay, Jodi Girouard writes about regaining a sense of hope while staying at a peer-run respite: "There I found peace in the valley by the river. I learned to throw river rocks into the water and release my pain and hurt from the men who took part of my life."

Navigating paternalism

When we navigate the psychiatric system, we often run up against what's called "medical paternalism," which is when healthcare providers make decisions on our behalf, supposedly acting for our own good. This can shut us out of that decision-making process, and losing our ability to make our own decisions can be traumatic.

Several of these stories describe a power imbalance between patient and provider. Some providers in these stories dismiss patients' concerns; some withhold needed information about treatments.

Some of our contributors had similar experiences of being prescribed medications with intolerable effects. The anonymous author of "Brain Blender" describes meetings with doctors who didn't listen when told the medications were not working. "Every conversation I had about medication during this period could be summed up as: doctors trying to convince me the side effects were a necessary evil, or that I was lying about them," says this writer. Some writers mentioned withdrawal when coming off of their meds. We also had contributors who finally, after trial and error, found drugs that helped them. Others found life without medication to be their best option.

Two of the authors wrote about how adults in their lives taught them about risk. They were told their bodies and behaviors needed to be controlled or something bad would happen. The Borderline Academic describes being called to the headmaster's office at school. There, she was scolded for trying to find a special connection with a teacher. She was told this teacher needed to be protected from her. "We don't know what could happen if we don't put a stop to this behavior," the headmaster told her. Malaika Puffer writes about being shamed, and even restrained, for harming herself. As a result, she came to believe that she was both sick and a moral failure. "I was victim and perpetrator, a closed system," she writes.

Finding meaning

Many of these stories are about finding the meaning behind our extreme states. The psychiatric system often tells us that our states are symptoms of illness. But many of us have needed answers beyond mere pathology. Our contributors found that meaning through various channels: poetry, filmmaking, activism, academia, and friendship.

Kaz DeWolfe writes of finding a spiritual community of people who had visions and heard voices—and who found meaning in them. Instead of their visions and voices being symptoms of brokenness, they were gifts of magick. "We interpreted each other's dreams and visions. We created spells to help navigate life's stressors and survive oppressive forces in our world. We worked through trauma together. We raised healing energy to fill painful emotional voids left by sexual assault, child abuse, and neglect."

Calvin Rey Moen concludes his essay with the recognition that his feelings of detachment and misplaced anger had their roots in abuse and trauma. He also attributes this understanding to being part of a community of peers. "We recognize abusive dynamics and the effects of trauma. We connect our big feelings and responses to bigger systems we are forced to survive: classism and heterosexism and patriarchy and so much more. And I wonder, what if I had a community like this when I was young and trying to make sense of my demons?"

Contributors wrote from Vermont and beyond. They responded to our call for submissions in spite of its very short deadline. They quickly worked with us on revisions to finish this project within the time frame. We knew and had worked with some of the contributors. Others were people we'd never met, who saw a Facebook post or got an email from the Vermont Psychiatric Survivors mailing list. Many of them told us how challenging it was to write these stories. A few declined to use their names, or used pseudonyms, in order to preserve careers or relationships. All of them were incredibly vulnerable and brave experts on their own experiences.

In addition to personal essays, this book also includes a resource guide. We have listed a few groups, articles, and other media we have found useful. We believe that first-hand experience is its own expertise. Still, it sometimes helps to have academic studies to back up what we know to be true. And, as many writers express over and over in these pages, finding a community that won't judge us can be a key to our survival. Making meaning of our experiences can be crucial to advocating for ourselves.

In addition to creating a resource we hope will help someone feel less alone, editing this book was also an opportunity for us. We were able to make new connections. We got to know each other and ourselves more intimately. We deepened conversations about what it means to pass as sane, to what extent our extreme states could be gifts or curses, and what it is about them that really scares people.

Reading this guide might bring up strong feelings in psychiatric survivors, parents, friends and partners, and providers. We hope you have, or can find, support to express those feelings and process whatever comes up. Strong feelings can be a catalyst for change, and a crisis can be a vehicle for transformation.

As Emily Dickinson wrote, "Much Madness is divinest Sense — / To a discerning Eye —" Learning to discern what Madness is telling us is a lifelong task.

—Kaz DeWolfe and Calvin Rey Moen, editors

Children Don't Belong in Cages

Jolie Mahan

I know what it's like to be stuck in a cage. I've felt the bitterness of relentless boredom, the desperate isolation that could make me turn to inanimate objects for company, the tortured powerlessness that comes with not knowing if or when I'd ever be free again. I've had to peer out of a barred window at a frigid upstate winter, watching the snow pile up on an abandoned bicycle in the hospital courtyard day after day, wondering who could've left it there and forgotten about it. Didn't they know a child could see it from their miserable, confined quarters, longing for the day they could ride a bike again, not knowing how many days, weeks, or months it would be until they could breathe fresh air instead of the stagnant, sterile air of the psych ward?

When I arrived at the hospital for the second time, I was kept in a room with a camera. The live feed was displayed on a small television in the nurse's station where everyone, patient or visitor, could see it.

I felt like an animal on display, like a hamster in a tank that anyone's curious eyes could inspect for their own amusement. For days I had no privacy, living with the perpetual feeling of being watched and studied. Eventually I was moved into a general room with a roommate, once a new person came onto the ward who they thought needed the surveillance more than I did.

As painful as it is to be kept in a cage, there's nothing like the sympathetic pain of witnessing another child being kept in one. I could hear the girl who was in that room screaming incoherently every night, just frantic, terrified screaming. I remember once seeing her strapped to a table and then wheeled back into that room, likely forcefully injected with something to make her quiet.

She wasn't the only one who struggled with the staff during my stay. One girl tried to escape the ward, and she, too, was confined to the "safe room," a small room with padded walls and floor that kids in crisis were locked up in to keep them safe, or maybe as punishment for bad behavior. It was never clear which.

A fifteen-year-old roommate of mine came back from a home visit sobbing from panic and anxiety because hospital staff were demanding to strip-search her out of alleged concern for her safety and everyone else's. I tried to comfort her as much as I could, but she ended up grudgingly accepting their demands. After witnessing my friend so distraught by the process, I later refused to take a drug that could potentially cause a rash because they claimed I'd need to be stripped and inspected before and after starting it. She and I became close friends while we roomed together, and we often had to support each other during incredibly stressful times, including newly discovered problems with my physical health.

My vitals were taken daily, just like everyone else's. On the first or second day I was there, a nurse took my pulse and asked me if I knew I had an irregular heartbeat. I was unaware of any tachycardia in my history, but after a blood test I was quickly diagnosed with Grave's Disease—autoimmune hyperthyroidism—a condition that meant my thyroid was overactive because my immune system was attacking it. It's a disease that very few adolescents are diagnosed with. Not only was it affecting my heart by making it beat irregularly and way too fast, but it could also cause severe anxiety, psychosis, and fatigue, which I had previously thought to be a part of depression. In the same hospital visit, I was diagnosed with bipolar disorder and Grave's Disease and then had to undergo the brutally uncomfortable process of being medicated for both. I was miserable. My family says that when they visited me, I was in a zombie-like state and barely responsive.

The only emotional support I got when I was in the hospital that was truly beneficial, other than from the regular visits I had with my family, came entirely from other patients there. Looking for friends to share meals and pass the time, I found a group of four other kids who called themselves the "Fortified Milkshake Crew" (FMC) because of the nutrition shakes that one bulimic member was forced to have at every meal. In order to be part of the group, I had to sip her drink like the rest of them, a ritual we considered rooted more in solidarity than hazing. After meals, she had to sit outside in the hallway to digest, and I would happily hang out of my doorway to talk to her, eager to escape the constant gaze of the camera. We became very close friends, and after we were discharged we exchanged contact info—something we were expressly forbidden to do. The two of us and one other FMC member remained best friends for some time. It ended up being one of the wisest choices we ever made because, as we soon found out, the struggles of living with mental illness don't end in the hospital. They were only just beginning.

When I was discharged from the hospital, I still had to go back daily for a period of "partial hospitalization" where I did all of my schoolwork. Then I started going to school at a therapeutic day program after getting an individualized education program (IEP), which described me as "emotionally disturbed." There were six kids in each class, an aide, and a teacher. All of the other kids had IEPs, emotional struggles, and learning disorders of various sorts. We were expected to work on our mental health and were never assigned homework. We were never expected to be academic achievers at all, really. Before my health crisis, I was in advanced math and science classes, hoping to go to college to become a software engineer, but none of those classes were accessible to me anymore.

Neither was a school band. The clarinet I'd started playing in fourth grade had been a refuge during periods of intense anguish related to the struggle I was having with my gender identity. I was bullied for dressing in boy clothes, and when I cut my hair very short and presented as a tomboy, I was called a dyke. On days when I couldn't stand the thought of eating lunch in the cafeteria, I would go to a practice room and play my clarinet. After I switched schools, I tried returning by bus several times a week to continue playing in band. But the bullying didn't stop when I changed schools, especially since it mostly took place online. One person called the new school I went to "the crazy school for retards." I dropped out of band and the clubs I'd been a part of: the Gay-Straight Alliance and the history club. There were no extra-curricular activities at my new school, and it was much harder to form close relationships in a space where a quarter of the people were adult workers, professionals, and teachers.

I soon transferred to a different school with larger classes, one that wasn't just for kids with IEPs but for those who were truants, teen moms, and other people who weren't violent but didn't follow all the rules. Lots of us were rebels and stoners. Having an art class with a lot of freedom to explore made us a very artistic bunch. I studied computer animation while my friends learned about photography and made pinhole cameras. Gym took place in the same room as our cafeteria, the basement of a rented church, and sometimes physical education was just walking outside around the neighborhood. After we were moved out of the church into a wing of a public high school, we were forced to undergo the humiliation of being herded through the halls to the gymnasium. We were aware of our reputation as "bad kids," but yet again I managed to survive in another group of close-knit friends. This time we were the Flesh-Eating Four, and all our imagined personas—Cannibal, Zombie, Ghost, and mine, Mutant—were a playful defense against the stigma we all sometimes felt, as people who were supposedly more dangerous than the average person. Having that kind of relationship with other people who were in the same place, engaging in struggle with them, and supporting each other was the most important thing I ever did for my mental health.

Some of the institutions I was in and out of had strict rules not to socialize with the other children outside of the program. It was a rule I frequently broke, and I'm glad I did because some of the kids who go through these systems live painfully short lives. I found that out when I was a senior in high school and a friend from the therapeutic day program died suddenly. I have enormous sympathy for the kids who endure their friends' deaths, whether from overdose, suicide, violence, or illness. It's cruel to expect kids to endure it in isolation from other struggling adolescents, completely dependent on their families and adult professionals for care. They're seen as totally incompetent to care for themselves and others, but in reality, struggling teens are in the best position to help other struggling teens.

We should be creating community-based institutions that don't involve caging and forced treatment, where kids are encouraged to help each other and form supportive networks to collectively better their social and mental positions. We should be promoting spaces that involve skill-sharing and cooperation to build foundations for growth instead of insisting on "self-care," therapy, and medication as panaceas for mental health. To be a truly mentally healthy person at any age, we need the autonomy to choose who we spend our time with, and the freedom to do so. Depending on solutions that prevent kids from engaging with one another and encourage distrust of mentally ill people for emotional support will likely lead to dysfunctional adults with internalized mentalism and dis/ableism, instead of promoting long-term healing and growth.

For the last several years, I've been learning about cages and about how the world we live in depends on them to "disappear" problems by disappearing people. I think about how caging people often doesn't make them better and often makes them a lot worse. If incarcerating a person in a cage is viewed as justifiable punishment, how can keeping a child in a cage be part of their healing? I believe that both situations are almost always unnecessarily cruel, and there are far better solutions for people who have had problematic behavior, whether they are convicted of crimes, have harmed other people, or are living with mental illness and are much more likely to hurt themselves than others. Cages can't end violence; they often help create it. Similarly, cages can't cure mental illness; they often help perpetuate it. Any future I can imagine with more peace, less mental illness, and less violence is one that has millions fewer people in cages.

From the poem "So Many Ways to Be Beautiful"

what if we finished what we started what if we brought the pigs down what if we wrote the books that no one else is writing about the lives we are still living the bodies we are still loving the signals we are crossing the men at the border the women on the street the people with mismatched pronouns and fucked up hair the people with bound breasts pink heels striped pants gender dysphoria and so many ways to be beautiful that only the schoolchildren can find the names. what if. what if we brought our gospel home.

—Jacks McNamara

Brain Blender

Anonymous[*]

There was a hurricane of shrapnel in my skull. I don't mean that literally, nor am I using it as a metaphor for some kind of inner turmoil. I'm struggling to describe a physical sensation that dominated my life for five years, between the ages of sixteen and twenty-two. It included huge rises and drops in pressure, like my skull was being inflated and deflated. I was haunted by an awareness of a point at the center of my brain that had spikes radiating out and scraping my braincase. There was movement, as if my brain was physically spinning inside my skull like a spherical compass jerking around in a falling airplane.

I have never been able to categorize the feeling. It was both incredibly vivid and obviously impossible. Whenever "the sensation" came, my visual perception seemed to sharpen. I was terrified and overwhelmed by the disgusting amount of detail apparent in peo-

---

[*] *Author's name withheld by request.*

ple's teeth and skin. I had a coinciding urge to hurt my hands, which I sometimes sated by punching things, and other times by smashing my one hand with a heavy object held in the other.

It is the single worst thing I've ever felt, and it occurred when I was being accused of something, when I was overwhelmed by a task, and when I felt like I had no control or agency. When "the sensation" came, I found myself unable to think critically or communicate. My only defense against it was to extricate myself from the situation and seek privacy until it ended. My mother would follow me wherever I ran, screaming that I couldn't hide from my problems. I was never able to communicate to her what was happening because she made a point of discounting anything I said while my voice was raised.

I learned that the only way to get her to leave was to escalate my behavior and scare her, so I started destroying my possessions. It served a dual purpose: mostly it got her to leave, and I was convinced that cathartic destruction could rip my brain out of the sensation. My car was a mess of bloody dents, the drywall in my room was swiss cheese, and my hands were constantly raw and aching. This strategy worked more often than not, and when she left I would lie down on the ground and yell at my brain to stop the sensation.

Usually I would yell to exhaustion and fall into a stupor for the rest of the day.

I started to realize that the sensation came only when I felt put-upon by someone with power over me. Just as I started to realize this, my mother gave me an ultimatum: either I would lose my car and all financial support, or I had to check into an inpatient psych unit "voluntarily" and stay until the doctor said I was stable or improving. She repeated this ultimatum on many occasions. Most of those times, I moved out of the house and stayed with a friend or significant other. Four of those times, I acquiesced and checked myself into a psychiatric hospital.

There are several factors inherent in the current model of inpatient treatment that drastically increased the difficulty of effectively communicating my needs to staff.

Barriers to Self-Advocacy That I Faced

1. Confirmation Bias

Confirmation bias is the human tendency to interpret new information in a way that confirms one's existing beliefs and hypotheses.

I was, and am, very receptive to the idea of taking medication that makes life manageable, but without exception all of the medications I was given during this time had absolutely intolerable side effects. I can't deal with negative changes to balance, coordination, sexual function, and speed of thought. If any of these are impaired by medication, I experience an overwhelming sense of panic and loss of control that I've never felt outside of the context of psych drugs.

Because of this sensitivity, every time I went to the hospital the staff was told by multiple sources that I was "resistant to drugs." This made it near impossible to explain why a specific medication was not working for me. Every conversation I had about medication during this period could be summed up as: doctors trying to convince me the side effects were a necessary evil, or that I was lying about them.

2. Medicating to Docility, not Wellness

The main problem I had with my overwhelming sensations was that they impaired my ability to communicate, problem-solve, and achieve my goals. The doctors I met with during this part of my life saw my yelling and punching walls as the main problem. A patient's inner experience cannot be observed, patients' self-reporting is not taken seriously, and loud events are memorable. All of these factors contribute to a system where a patient suffering quietly 100% of the time is considered an improvement over a patient suffering loudly 10% of the time.

No one believed me when I said things were worse on hardcore antipsychotics. Doctors often concluded I was confused and not remembering correctly.

"You *say* things are worse, but remember a week ago when you were hitting things?"

3. Ignoring the Stimulus of the Locked Unit

Before checking into a psych ward, I experienced my extreme sensation and the resulting outbursts at most once a week, and always as a result of an interaction with my mother or as a response to a seemingly hopeless task. On a psych unit, I was overwhelmed by the sensation at least once every day, and I exploded (punching walls, screaming at people) about every other day.

I started to realize that the solution to my problems might be mostly found in building a life with less of the stimulus that caused this sensation, but I found it impossible to convince doctors that the outbursts they were observing were unusual in their intensity and frequency. Because they knew I was admitted for explosive episodes, and because that was what they observed on the unit, it was seen as a baseline in a way that I feel was diagnostically invalid.

A locked unit is an environment unlike normal civilian life in every way. People respond differently to this change in stimulus. Some people respond violently to having their freedom taken away; some people suffer internally from it and withdraw into silence. A person who speaks with the same dialect and communication style as the staff will find themselves feeling less isolated and misunderstood than a person whose speech differs from the staff. I could list examples forever.

Because of this, the notion that observed behavior on a locked unit is consistently indicative of a patient's ability to thrive in civil society is absurd.

4. The Credibility Gap

This is the big one. Effective psychiatric treatment requires consent and effective communication between doctor and patient. Being a patient on a locked unit immediately robbed me of credibility. The staff considered everything I said as a possible lie or delusion. I can say without a fraction of a doubt that I have never experienced suspicion, distrust, and patronization to the degree I experienced them at the various psychiatric units in Vermont and New Hampshire.

This lack of trust immediately put me on edge—every moment of communication was like being on a debate stage. I had to consider not only what the truth was but how to get my audience to understand it, how to reinforce my credibility, how to defuse prejudices they may have, and how to avoid statements and styles of communication that staff associate with "crazy people."

Walking the Tightrope

All four occasions of being admitted to a psych hospital, staying until the doctors "found a medication that worked for me," and then telling my mother that I was "doing better" were bullshit. Each time, I basically pulled off a ruse so I could avoid homelessness. Even though I was legally voluntarily admitted, if I left without my mother's permission she would render me homeless and take my car away. Because of this context, and because of the factors listed above that made honest communication and therapeutic treatment impossible, the hospital instead was basically an acting test—the prize for passing it was freedom.

I realized that, however unfair it was, I had to present a face they would see as sane despite their prejudices and biases. I didn't describe the head sensa-

29

tion at all, or I "clarified" that it was just rhetorical hyperbole. I realized I would not be able to communicate my medication concerns or have them taken seriously, so I decided to suffer through whatever doped-up feelings or side effects the medication caused and then stop taking it when I left. I realized that my extreme unease at being on a locked unit would never be considered, so I isolated myself by pretending to have gastric distress, and I learned how to dissociate when the sensation came during conversations with doctors.

The bathroom strategy worked much better on units, because at home my mother would follow me and scream through the bathroom door, which unit staff never did. The second strategy (pretending I was elsewhere) had the side effect of presenting me as slow and spacey, but, because all they cared about were the explosive episodes, it didn't matter. This skill might be an unhealthy adaptation, but I hold that it's the most valuable thing I learned on a locked unit. That said, it's horrible that I had to learn to dissociate to prove my "sanity." But when a system is dysfunctional or fails people, they will adapt with extraordinary measures to have their needs met.

I still wanted help. I still needed tools to protect myself from the head sensation and its associated episodes. But the inpatient psych system was unable to provide those tools.

How I "Got Better"

The single largest factor in my freedom from domination by the maddening cranial sensation was support from a friend. A video editing colleague let me live in her apartment for an entire year after my last hospitalization. She was the only person who recognized that all of my episodes came in response to interactions with unreasonable authority—mostly my mother—during which I felt powerless and hopeless. She encouraged me to finish my education and negotiate freelance jobs, and she helped me build a filmmaking crew. While living with her, the sensation's frequency immediately reduced. I was becoming overwhelmed by it, at most, once a month.

By working on goals that I chose, my feeling of worth increased, and I was less overwhelmed by tasks and challenges. Through freelance video work, I learned to communicate better, manage troublesome relationships, and deal with irrational and unfair authority figures. I found that with reduced contact with my mother, I could interact with her calmly and functionally. I also realized the way she treated me was abusive and wrong. I struggle to this day to reconcile my familial bond with the gravity of her abuses.

As the stakes and complexity of the video work increased, I decided to try medication again. This time, my experience with doctors was very different. The confirmation bias problem was incredibly lessened by not having my mother or emergency department staff give the doctor their opinion. Because I didn't mention the sensation or outbursts at all, I was able to negotiate for medication that helped me achieve my goals, rather than zombify me. Because I was an adult seeking voluntary help from a psychiatrist, his opinion of my baseline was not affected by observing me on a locked unit. Finally, because I had a college education and a stable job, I had enough credibility for the doctor to immediately hear and consider what I was saying.

One thing I am sure of is that I did not, at any point, have a mental problem that could be solved by our inpatient system. Were it not for my ability to strategize, were it not for my colleague's generosity, I no doubt would still be in and out of psych wards, punching walls and yelling at people to leave me alone because my brain feels like it's being ripped to shreds by a tornado of nails.

I know there are people much like me stuck on locked units, people who have extreme and frightening responses to extraordinary and difficult life situations, and whose responses landed them on a locked unit where they remain as their condition worsens. Many of these people do not have the privileges and luck I had to afford them the tools to escape that loop. I am convinced most of them would thrive if the system would focus on helping them achieve independence and freedom from the circumstances that trigger their pathologized behaviors, rather than treating the behaviors as if they exist in a vacuum.

We need to ask these people what their biggest challenges are. I believe that everyone is an expert on their own lives. Very few people truly do not know what the barriers in their world are. Mostly those trying to help them are just asking the wrong questions, or not really asking questions at all.

From "Notes on the Unfathomable"

The Borderline Academic

I had been chosen for the exercise because of my size. Because I was the smallest person in the room. And still, I wasn't small enough. No matter what, I couldn't make myself small enough. I couldn't make myself disappear. This is the border between anorexia and suicidality. This is the border between madness, sexuality, femaleness, and lack of restraint. This is what it means to be a borderline. On the borderline. To not be able to make yourself disappear.

***

Notes on Knowledge/Insight:

Knowledge = a form of power.

Knowledge = restraint.

If a person who lacks restraint KNOWS they lack restraint and ADMITS they lack restraint, we are less afraid of them.

In admitting that they lack restraint, they transfer the knowledge of their lack of restraint to US (we/us = general public, other people in their life).

A person who lacks restraint = mysterious, scary, unpredictable.

In some way, this is power. This is dangerous—predatory. They lack restraint and we don't know what's going on in their head. We don't know when they will lash out, manipulate us, be violent.

If they ADMIT they lack restraint, then we KNOW. We KNOW what's going on in their head.

Our knowledge = power over them.

***

I'm at a Hearing Voices training, and we're learning about an exercise called "family sculpts." A voice hearer, Kristy, stands at the center of the circle and selects participants to play the roles of members of her family, arranging them into a configuration that best reflects her view of the family dynamics.

It's time to select someone to play herself. "I need someone who's small," she says. "I need to be able to show how small and powerless I felt as a child."

Inevitably, she looks straight at me. I am five feet flat and one hundred pounds. "You're the smallest," she says. "Come act the part of me." Others in the room laugh. I show my teeth, force a laugh. It's supposed to be funny. I'm used to this.

I stand up, come to the center of the room, wait for her to place me in the arrangement. She opens her mouth to speak but then pauses. "Hmm," she says. "Well—uh. I was going to ask you to lie down in a fetal position to represent how powerless I felt in my family...but you're in a dress."

I laugh nervously.

The trainer interjects. "That's okay," she says. "You can ask her to lie down."

Kristy laughs. "Well, I mean, I want to protect her dignity."

"You didn't have any dignity when you were a child, did you?" the trainer asks. Kristy shakes her head.

I lie down in a fetal position. Immediately, half the students in the room begin to giggle. One woman hands me her suit jacket. "You should probably use this. To...protect your dignity." I place it over my legs. After a brief, awkward moment, the exercise moves on, and Kristy begins to select more participants to play other members of her family.

For the rest of the exercise, I try to be as still as possible. *If I am frozen, maybe they won't see me*, I think. After a minute or so, I realize that my teeth are chattering and my hands are shaking. I bite my lips and dig my nails into my palm. *Don't let it show*, I tell myself. I wait and wait for the exercise to be over. *Please don't let me draw attention to myself, please don't let me move in any way that makes people notice me*, I pray silently.

After the exercise is over and the participants are allowed to return to their seats, I rush out of the room and sprint to the bathroom. Inside the stall, I text one of my closest friends. "I don't know what's wrong with me," I type. "I just know it's going to be seen as a come on. I know it's going to look like I was trying to get sexual attention. Like I was trying to flaunt my body or something. Like I was flashing some of the men in the training on purpose to get their attention. Like I'm delusional." At this point, tears are streaming down my face. "I hate having a body, I hate it so much. I feel like I can't move around in space without being seen as a predator. And what if I am? What if, by virtue of having a body, my body, I am a predator?"

I conclude with a line that, by this point, I've gotten rather used to repeating: "See? I told you. I'm permanently screwed up."

***

For the record, I was, indeed, wildly in love with him. The way I thought about him felt BIG, HUGE, GIGANTIC, beyond what anyone else could possibly understand. I was obsessed with him. It was intense. I thought of him constantly and continuously. When I woke up, when I fell asleep, during every task of my daily life. I fantasized about him—sexually, romantically. It was all-consuming. I admired him—his coffee brown hair, his mischievous smile, his deep laugh, his confidence, his intelligence, his willingness to listen. He was the first person to ever make me feel truly valued—beyond just a series of accomplishments, or my GPA—but for me as a person, for my hopes and dreams and desires. I wanted to be his favorite person. I yearned, desperately, for him to think about me as much as I thought about him. I would've done just about anything for his attention.

I was fifteen. Isn't that how love is supposed to be when you are fifteen?

I would wait outside his classroom door so that I could "accidentally" run into him when he finished teaching a class. I came up with lists of questions about Spanish grammar I just had to ask and set up appointments to meet him in his office. I wrote novels that dramatized some of the hard stuff I was going through in high school and shared them with him. "They're just fiction," I would say, hoping, praying he would doubt me. I asked him to partner with me in forming a "Spanish table" where students could practice their Spanish at lunch, secretly knowing that I would be the only student who showed up. I would cry in his office. I would cry if he was talking to other students in his office.

After a year or so, when I was seventeen, he began to avoid me. He made excuses for why I could no longer set up appointments with him in his office. He cancelled Spanish table due to lack of student interest (which hadn't been an issue before). I didn't understand what was going on. I didn't understand why he was suddenly withdrawing his attention.

I don't know. Maybe I did understand. Maybe I understood perfectly. Maybe, deep down, I really, truly did understand but I didn't want to. I just know I hated myself and blamed myself. I had ruined a good thing.

I began to stand outside his office and cry some more. I cried during his class. I wanted him to notice me, to sympathize with me again like he had before, to care about me. I would come back to my dorm room and cry and cry. One of my friends saw me crying every day and decided to write him an email. "My friend feels like you are avoiding her," she said. "She is going through such a hard time. She is being bullied in school, and her parents don't understand at all. Can you please just talk to her again? Can you please be there for her? You're the only one who gets it."

And that, my friends, is how this writer—this former award-winning, 4.0 GPA-earning high school student—ended up in the headmaster's office.

***

If a person lacks restraint, we want them to confess to lacking restraint.
The first step of AA = admitting powerlessness.
"Schizophrenics" are said to "lack insight"—they need to "admit"/"confess" to having an illness.
We need to gain back power through their admission/confession.
Their lack of restraint is much scarier/more unbridled/unrestrained if we don't have knowledge of it.
It may also be much scarier/more unbridled/unrestrained if they themselves don't have knowledge of it (if they have knowledge of it, then it is more cold and calculating, which is still dangerous but more acceptable/predictable—it

is kind of "badass," versus the crazy, unrestrained, uncontrollable Mad person).

***

My headmaster was a British man with a long beard who sat perfectly rigidly upright in the boardroom. I sat across from him at the table, cowering. My body was doing the shaking thing. I was trying to make myself small.

"This is a very personal, intimate part of your life that you need to be honest with yourself about. You have some very inappropriate feelings for your Spanish teacher. Very. Inappropriate. You are crying in his office, you are seeking attention, you have engaged in self-harm. It is very clear that you are willing to go to quite some extreme lengths to receive special attention. From now on, you won't be rewarded for that. You'll be treated just like any other student. These feelings must be put an end to."

My parents sat on either side of me. I wanted to disappear.

"I need to protect the safety and well-being of the employees within this institution. Your crying publicly, your crying in a male employee's office, your feelings—do you know how this looks? The appearance of impropriety—that is enough to destroy an instructor's livelihood. Your actions show a disregard for this man's well-being. And I need to put an end to that. To protect him."

He paused, sighing disgustedly.

"We don't know what could happen if we don't put a stop to this behavior. We don't know, for example, if you would be willing to make up a story—to conjure up an accusation—to get some sort of revenge. We don't know if you would say that Sr. Smith had, for example, been sexually inappropriate to you. We just don't know. And that is why we need to get your behavior under control."

***

This aligns with Melanie Yergeau's work: autistic be-
    haviors are usually presumed to be uncon-
    scious/unintentional. Intentionally claiming an
    autistic identity makes space for autistic behav-
    iors to be an intentional form of communication
    that takes agency.
Same with claiming a Mad identity or a fat identity—
    instead of these things being unknowable, mys-
    terious traits, they are KNOWN to the individu-
    al and intentionally performed.
Does this unintentionally create disavowal and dis-
    tancing of ourselves from people who do lack

restraint? From behaviors that are genuinely un-restrained?

Does this send the message, "Being Mad is okay because I am CHOOSING to be Mad and performing being Mad, and because I KNOW I am Mad and I like it" and therefore the subtle message that those who don't know they are mad or are not choosing it/performing it as an intentional identity are less acceptable/less valuable?

Are Mad Pride and Autistic Pride the equivalent of tripping, saying, "I meant to do that," and then tripping some more?

Don't get me wrong. If it is, that's cool. We should be destigmatizing tripping. If tripping (= madness, autism) becomes an okay thing to do, an okay identity to perform, then by all means, let's do this shit.

But what about the people who really don't trip on purpose? Who are tripping all over themselves and aren't aware of it—it's totally accidental and not possible or feasible to perform or know as an identity? To "mean to do"? What then? Are there cases like this? Is it possible to make something acceptable or reclaim something without requiring its performance/chosenness as an identity?

***

Afterwards, I stood frozen, paralyzed, beside my locker for ten minutes. My whole body shook violently. Inside, I was numb.

Then, I went back to my dorm room, played Ke$ha's "Mr. Watson" on full volume from my computer speakers, and sang along at the top of my lungs. I made sure to leave my door open so that others would hear me.

Looking back at that moment, I sometimes ask myself, "What the hell was I doing?" And then I remember: what other option did I have?

Finding Community

Kaz DeWolfe

Growing up, I learned pretty quickly which things I could not talk to my parents about. I could not ever mention that I sometimes heard voices speaking to me while drifting off to sleep at night. I couldn't mention all the ways that sounds and words took form and augmented the colors in the space around me. It didn't make sense to anyone else. I couldn't mention the tiny, shimmering dots of color that filled the space between objects. No one else saw these tiny specks that were everywhere I looked.

Any mention of perception or experience outside of the realm of normal, which my parents were the judges of, concerned them. If I said the wrong thing, my parents would seem quietly terrified of me. I could tell they were worried something was *wrong* with me, like something was wrong with my uncle Jonathan, who was diagnosed as schizoaffective.

I didn't have many visions or hear many voices for most of my childhood. Most of those experiences happened as I was falling asleep, so I could write them off as only dreams. My other odd sensory perceptions I could justify as poor eyesight, or part of the constellation of learning disabilities I was diagnosed with in elementary school. My parents were fine with us having learning disabilities, as long as we were working to overcome them through specialized instruction and daily stimulant use. ADHD and dyslexia did not carry the same weight or dread as a serious mental illness.

I found middle and high school to be overwhelmingly distressing and traumatic. I was bullied by my classmates. I was sexually harassed and assaulted and told no one. I had frequent panic meltdowns. I cried so hard it hurt and hyperventilated until I nearly fainted. I was terrified to let my parents know how much emotional pain I was in, but I could no longer hide it.

They sent me to a psychiatrist, who diagnosed me with generalized anxiety disorder. He prescribed buspirone. I wasn't sure if the doctor or therapist would tell my parents what I said in our sessions, so I was never fully open or honest about my distress or the trauma I was living through. I never mentioned the voices I heard at night or my unusual belief that I had accidentally teleported into an alternate universe. I was absolutely sure that I didn't belong in this one at all.

When I got to college, I felt for the first time this little glimmer of freedom. I befriended other oddball creative and queer students, some of whom were open and unashamed about their psych diagnoses. But I still found it hard to identify as a mentally ill person, even when I started taking three different psych drugs daily. I experimented with telling people, "I have a mental illness," and then immediately panicked that I would be punished by unseen forces echoing my father's anger and judgement.

One of my new creative college friends was a witch. She introduced me to a whole community of people who had visions, heard voices, and perceived magick and energy, and no one in the community thought they were damaged for it. I may not have been able to identify as a mentally ill person, but at nineteen years old, I found that I was more than happy to identify as a witch. I was downright magical, and for the first time in my life I got to celebrate it.

I'm not interested in prescribing spirituality or religion to all young people experiencing extreme states. While I was able to find a spiritual practice and a community that I benefited from, I am all too aware of the abuse that can happen in any spiritual or religious group.

But there were certainly things about this particular community of witches—a coven of mixed-age individuals that met at a few witches' homes—that was hugely supportive to me in those early days of my madness. It was the first time in my life that it felt safe to tell people honestly what I was thinking, feeling, and experiencing. My coven siblings saw me as gifted, not broken and in need of fixing.

It was immensely valuable to me to have people in my life who saw my experiences as meaningful and insightful, and not just symptoms. In rituals and gatherings, those shimmering dots inhabiting the negative space I had seen my whole life began to take form. I began to understand them as the way I visualize magick. The coven held space for all of our experiences of magick, validating each other and finding value in each other's perceptions.

We interpreted each other's dreams and visions. We created spells to help navigate life's stressors and survive oppressive forces in our world. We worked through trauma together. We raised healing energy to fill painful emotional voids left by sexual assault, child abuse, and neglect.

I was also able to explore my own gender fluidity and gender uncertainty within a spiritual and sacred framework. The coven was a delightfully queer-friendly space. I was able to openly explore the masculine and feminine depths within myself. (I later learned that many neopagan communities are not safe spaces for trans and gender-nonconforming individuals.)

I had a supportive community that allowed me to find meaning in my experiences and get support around life stressors, but I continued to experience distress throughout my college years. The pressures of academia and the challenges of interpersonal relationships were often more than I could handle.

I often went days without sleeping, desperately trying to keep up with my coursework. I had huge conflicts with my closest friends and romantic partners, lashing out angrily at times. At one point I screamed at an entire classroom of students who had ridiculed my work. I was lucky that I was never sectioned (admitted for emergency evaluation) or expelled in college (which regularly happens to students experiencing extreme states).

I saw a psychiatrist, who prescribed me Adderall to help me study and Cymbalta for depression. I had taken stimulants already and knew what to expect from them, but Cymbalta was an entirely new experience. I felt cut off from my body. I felt like a floating brain. The way I moved across campus was to point myself in a direction and drift that way, as though I was an astronaut in a spacesuit.

When I accidentally missed doses, I got intense electrical zapping sensations inside my head. I talked to my doctor about this, and he didn't think it was related to the drug at all. Years later, I learned that these "brain zaps" are entirely common when withdrawing from antidepressants and other psych drugs.

The doctor kept increasing my dosage, even though I was telling him the side effects were unbearable. But he insisted, based on my description of my despair, that I had major depression. He described it as a "serious brain disease" requiring medication. He was very excited about Cymbalta. It was fairly new, and he said it was extremely promising. He was sure that if I stuck with it, the side effects would decrease and I would find it beneficial to my mental health.

At some point I gave up hope of that ever happening and took myself off all my meds. After some weeks of withdrawal causing brain zaps and mood swings, I finally began to feel better. I wish I had known then to taper down slowly to minimize withdrawal effects.

Despite the unhelpful medication, and with support from my coven, I managed to get through college without being expelled or locked up in a psych unit. After graduation, I didn't want to leave my coven, so I found a job in the same city where I went to school.

A couple of years later, I fell madly in love with someone I had just met and impulsively married him only weeks after meeting. Like many whirlwind romances, this relationship quickly became volatile and abusive.

I tried to escape and turned to the witches for support. But when I got away and got to them, I found I couldn't open up about the abuse. The words stuck in my throat. I stayed quiet.

I think part of the ideology of the witchcraft we practiced made me fear they would blame me in some way for what was happening to me. Many of the witches believed in the "law of attraction," which is very frequently used to shame victims for "attracting" mistreatment and abuse. Some proponents of this "law" believe that all that is required to not be a victim is to have the right positive mindset and energy. Some believed in a universe that was ultimately good and just, and that people basically get what they deserve. They believed in the "Rule of Three," that whatever energy we put into the universe comes back to us with three times the intensity. Put out good vibrations, and get good things in return. Put out negative energy, or perhaps harmful words or deeds, and get three times as much negativity and harm.

I worried that the abuse in my marriage was just the universe paying me a debt I was owed for sometimes spreading negative energy and anger. Or at least I worried that the witches, who were my only hope for support, would quietly think that I deserved what was happening to me. So, I was silent for three years, and in those years I became spiritually dead inside. There was no magick, no healing energy. There was only cold reality full of pain and despair.

Without a support system, and after years of abuse, I ended up hospitalized a few times on locked psychiatric units. Each time was violent and traumatic.

Today, I again have visions and hear voices, but I don't ever feel the sense of spiritual bliss and connection with nature and the universe that I felt prior to my traumatizing marriage and traumatizing hospitalizations.

Instead, my visions often expose violent and oppressive social constructs. I see the gods of Western civilization and corporatism as giant, terrifying architecture and machinery. I see oppression such as racism, classism, cisheterosexism, and medical paternalism as physical structures. They fill our spaces and constrict our movement and words. I see them, and I try to carve out spaces free from their influence. It's exhausting work. I can't do it alone.

I no longer have a coven of witches, but I do have a community that values me and my perceptions. I have found a home in the Mad Pride movement and peer workforce. I have befriended Mad scholars: people with lived experience who are researching methods for supporting people in distress, from *our* perspective, rather than from an outsider, sane-privileged perspective. The Mad community largely provides the type of acceptance and support I sought in my college years.

When I look back on my history of extreme states, I have to conclude that a nonjudgmental and noncoercive community where I can be open and honest is the most valuable support to get me through difficult times. I have a need to talk about and find meaning in my experiences.

Psychiatric drugs have been a mixed bag, sometimes helpful and sometimes harmful. I currently take a low dose of a neuroleptic to dial back voices that became too distracting. Some people find antipsychotics to be unhelpful or even extremely harmful. I fully support every person's right to informed consent and right to refuse medical treatment.

Unfortunately, we have a psychiatric and legal system that violently forces drugs on some Mad folks, while withholding needed medications from others. I hope our entire culture will shift so acceptance, validation, and noncoercive support are the front-line "treatments" for extreme states. And perhaps one day we will have a medical system with any number of drugs readily available, with informed consent, as options, just in case.

Within the Fields of Possibilities

Jodi Girouard

If I can stop one heart from breaking,
I shall not live in vain;
If I can ease one life the aching,
Or cool one pain,
Or help one fainting robin
Unto his nest again,
I shall not live in vain.
    —Emily Dickinson

Perhaps my sorrows can be strung together to form a light that leads to the brightness I now find in life. I still struggle with my mental illness, but I desire to live, to fight, to keep on as much as possible.

I was first diagnosed with my illness at seventeen: my first overdose, my first hospitalization. Over the next thirty years I had forty visits as an inpatient in psychiatric hospitals, and I have spent countless hours at day hospitals, group therapies, individual therapy, and respite homes to stay alive.

I used to think suicide was an escape. I didn't believe that, if I waited, time would change my mind. I couldn't wait that long. I wanted out. I wanted relief. I wanted it right that moment. I had not given credit to the joy found in moments beyond the pain, beyond the grief, beyond the hardships of my illness.

I had forgotten there were many more moments of joy I possessed over the years of my illness. I have found days of sheer elation. Days of being a mother. Days of being recognized for my poetry, my stories, my voice. Days of being married. Days of living in nature, taking in the scents of flowers, the beauty of such color I had been denied when inside the muted walls of a locked ward. Days I wouldn't have had if I had died.

In my early twenties I finished college and worked as an in-home teacher for mothers and pre-schoolers. I worked in the islands of Vermont. I went door to door to develop my caseload, and my car was my office. I tried to teach mothers to care for and educate their children in ways that were beneficial to the young children. Even without toys and books, a mother could learn to engage with her child whom she loved, and many did.

I also found much neglect and abuse of the children and sometimes of the mothers. It hurt my heart, and I wanted to take them all home. I was unrealistic and grew despairing. One afternoon in my car, I heard my first voices. Auditory hallucinations.

There was no one in the car with me. I was alone. I was frightened. I was young. The voices came more and more. I was terrified others would find out that I was hallucinating and lock me up again. I hid the symptoms. I tried to keep on, but I kept slipping into despair and fear. I grew more and more despondent.

My husband knew something was happening. My own trauma and sadness occupied my thoughts. The abuse my clients suffered had triggered the voices. I kept trying to help them, but the hallucinations were loud, commanding, ordering me to die. And I couldn't keep it hidden. I fell apart. I couldn't function and was soon hospitalized. My husband stayed by my side and supported me no matter what I was going through.

In the hospital, I was put on my first round of antipsychotics. They never "cured" me. I experienced lasting side effects and never truly healed. I spent many months doped up and discouraged. I was always tired. I lost hope. I grew impatient for help. Through the years of living with my illness, I have often thought of ending my life—but I am so thankful that I never died. I am so grateful I have given myself the chance to keep on and find moments of happiness that have been blessings.

I spent the next thirty years trying to find help to rid myself of the voices. They have never gone away. They were first triggered by the sadness in that job. I ended up on disability, working part time when I could.

I have spent too many years hiding. My illness is a part of me. It is a part that is hard to acknowledge, but is part of who I am. Perhaps because of my illness I have a deeper understanding of emotions and can understand others' pain more easily.

I have fought to be nobody but myself. To be just Jodi. Over the last few years I have opened up about my life. I no longer hide that I hear voices. I am me. I speak to groups, I share my poetry, I am open about my illness, and that has been the most helpful, the most healing for me.

I continue to try medications. I go to the hospital when I am too tired to continue. I still hear scary voices. I call them the "neighbors" and try to visualize the noise as someone through the wall in another apartment. Just a neighbor making noise. Sometimes it helps.

I went away to a peer support home in Rochester, Vermont, called Alyssum. There I found peace in the valley by the river. I learned to throw river rocks into the water and release my pain and hurt from the men who took part of my life. I regained hope, and as Emily Dickinson said:

"Hope" is the thing with feathers —
That perches in the soul —

And sings the tune without the words —
And never stops — at all —

While at Alyssum, I began my memoir, which I look forward to publishing. I continue to write my poetry and stories. I know I have strengths that the world needs. If I had given up when I was seventeen, or in my early twenties when I was in such pain, I would not have had the goodness, the joy, the happiness of life in even an ordinary day.

I will always struggle. I will always have that fear that leaps up into my heart, that freezes my mind and makes me automatically think maybe I shouldn't be alive. But I have also gained skills to reform my fear. To learn to breathe in and out in the agony of my sadness. For I have much more to do in life.

Suicide is an escape I desperately try to avoid. For it is a void that would make me disappear completely. I want to still fight, to stand, to live in the hardness, for there are many more days to discover and embrace and enjoy. I am determined to keep on, to be just Jodi. For Jodi has much to give, just like the person reading this.

Running Through Fields

We are all children
Running through the fields of life,

Some taking worn paths,
Some in tall grass,
Still others in wild flowers.
But we are all here,
Together,
Running through the fields of life.
And some,
The ones who see beyond the fields,
They shake themselves with laughter
And make chains of dandelions
To wear upon their heads,
Casting off shoes
To run barefoot
In the wide variety
Of possibilities.

Nightmares and Demons and Death? You're Fine.

Calvin Rey Moen

I have no memories of my parents together; it's like I woke up at age five in small-town Minnesota, with my dad and little brother, wondering where my mom was and aching every day she was gone. I would write her long letters I never sent. I didn't want to make her sad with how miserable I was.

I started to have vivid nightmares; in one, my dad was painstakingly slicing off my brother's head with a steak knife. When I told him to stop, he asked if I'd rather have my ear cut off. I said no, but I felt terribly guilty about not saving my brother's life by losing an ear. My dad wasn't a monster. He was a young, single parent doing his best. He did make me sit at the table until I finished my beets, but that hardly counts as child abuse.

Some of the nightmares happened when I was awake, like when I was in the back yard and some underground creature started tunneling toward me. I could see the mounds of dirt rising under the grass, and I heard a grunting sound. I screamed and ran, thinking a snake was attacking me (I was afraid of nature as a child and pretty ignorant about the creatures that lived in it). Adults later assured me it was just a harmless gopher hole, that there was nothing to be afraid of. When I looked for the evidence later, it was gone.

Don't be afraid. Don't cry. You're fine. Or the tricks to make me laugh: tickling, which I hated but which made me giggle from fear, or grinning at me while cooing, "Don't smiiiiii-iiiiile!" until I couldn't help but curl up the corners of my mouth. An involuntary reflex, like when the doctor hit my knee with that tiny rubber mallet and my leg shot out from the exam table.

Around this time, I started to feel detached from my surroundings. I stared into the bathroom mirror, trying to convince myself this face I saw was me. I unfocused my eyes until the patterned tile floor took on a third dimension and sunk far below me. I sat on the toilet, legs dangling over this pit, wondering if it was really me inside this body and if there was any way to know who or where I was. There was certainly no one I could ask such a question, even if I had words for it.

Eventually a judge told my parents they had to share custody of me and my brother, so we alternated school years and summers between them. At our dad's, I wrote in my journal in a secret code I invented and hid in my room a lot. I counted down the days until I could see our mom. At our mom's, we went to church.

That's only partly true. Her house was, itself, a church. We listened to sermons on cassette tapes while we did chores; secular (non-Christian) music was not allowed (except for a few artists my mom liked—we were both obsessed with Prince and Cyndi Lauper), and the TV was kept locked in a closet. Portraits of a white Jesus with soft hair and sorrowful eyes hung next to crosses on the walls, and mom spent hours a day praying audibly.

And we did go to church. We were part of a congregation of evangelicals who met weekly at the 4-H building to sing praises accompanied by guitar, piano, and tambourine; spontaneously prophesy; and weep openly, hands raised toward the ceiling. Newcomers were called upon to approach the front and accept Jesus as their savior. Born-again members were encouraged to be "filled with the Holy Spirit" and receive the gift of "tongues"—the ability to speak an unknown language.

Anyone who was sick or got out of line would have hands laid on them—as many believers' hands as could reach to touch some part of the afflicted person's body. The pastor would palm the person's forehead and pray, shouting, "In the name of Jesus!" to chase out any demon that dwelled within. This continued until the person received the healing—usually signaled by fainting into the arms of the group.

My skepticism and dissatisfaction with these practices accumulated over time, but it burst forth dramatically one Sunday when I was twelve or thirteen. I stood near the back of the row of folding chairs, singing along to "Send Down the Rain, Lord" and looking around at the other families. I knew these families, and I knew their secrets from the other kids in the youth group. Marriages seethed with bitterness, dads drank too much and shouted, teenagers had sex. In our own home, violent men were briefly part of our family and then gone. My mom regularly made out with the pastor in his car in our driveway. Normal enough stuff, but no one ever talked about it in the open. Praise the Lord.

And, in that moment, the blurry glow of God's glory dissipated like fog, and I saw a couple dozen rural white folks in a borrowed building working themselves into some sort of frenzy. I felt detached. Tambourines clanged hollowly. Someone sang off key.

I went to the bathroom to escape the sudden vertigo of the spell breaking. After I'd been gone long enough to rouse her suspicions, my mom found me. I confessed what I had seen—these rituals stripped of their meaning. She was hurt, angry. How could a child of hers be lost to Satan?

Our relationship was never the same after that. I became the reviled, know-it-all teenager. Who did I think I was to judge others? "Ye shall know them by their fruits," and my fruits were all rotten. My mom had been my lifeline until then, my main source of understanding and acceptance, and her disgust with me fueled outrage and despair that had no outlet. Her discipline became stricter and angrier. Whether it was for not brushing my teeth or being on drugs (I never was), her lectures were always sermons, and she was always right because, in our house, she spoke for God.

For a few more years, I still had to attend church, but I just stood, sat, and left. I was subjected to less frequent but more intense exorcisms, commanded to say the name "Jesus" but found that the name stuck in my throat. Their hands would all be on me until I surrendered to the spirit and allowed myself to fall to the floor—which I felt bad about faking, but otherwise the ordeal would go on indefinitely.

In my teens, I was befriended by other youth in the church, secret rebels and fornicators who glowed with the Spirit on Sunday morning after they glowed with 80-proof spirits on Saturday night. I was pretty square compared to them, but I did what I could to find acceptance and companionship, including finally agreeing to have sex with one of them, who was my boyfriend. He was controlling and threatening, making sure my mom kept me grounded throughout most of high school so I couldn't escape him, and this led to the first time I remember hearing voices while fully awake.

I was hiding from him in the basement, and I could hear my pulse, feel the blood sloshing through my veins. Then my heartbeat turned into a chant. It was cryptic at first; then, like pieces of a puzzle coming together, I made out the message: multiple voices demanded I spill my blood. I could feel them closing in. Could they force me to do it? Even though I no longer believed I was surrounded by evil spirits, I didn't know how to explain to myself what I heard and felt. I didn't know how to explain it to anyone else, either. Besides, who was I going to tell? My mom already thought I was on drugs.

When he found me, I tried to pretend I had just been sitting around relaxing in the dark basement next to the discarded vacuum cleaner. Not hiding. Of course not. Why would I? Then I think he made me have sex with him. I don't know. That part's a blur.

The day after I graduated from high school, a friend's pickup, containing the few things I could call mine, was in my mom's driveway. I was so relieved to move with my new, not-abusive boyfriend into our own apartment. We would have a comfy couch in front of an actual TV and listen to whatever music we wanted to. We were adult college students now.

But, a few months into living my dream life, I couldn't make sense of my fears. I convinced my boyfriend to move our bed underneath the bay window in the living room so I felt less trapped. In the summer, our apartment was infested with little roly-poly bugs, and I was so scared of them I became enraged. I didn't understand these feelings because my life was fine now. I had gotten away from the routines of violence, poverty, housing instability, hostility, and religious repression and was safe in my own home with a person I trusted.

Except I started to hate him for no reason, and the bathroom-tile detached feelings grew, and this time I tried to talk to a friend about it: "You know I don't believe in this, but I feel possessed. Like there is something not-me inside me trying to take over. I think it's going to try to kill me." She assured me this wasn't really happening and asked if I had talked to the campus mental health counselor.

I had, once, and left disappointed. She told me I seemed okay. I was getting good grades, working and paying rent, living with a sweet guy (who had given me flowers that day to cheer me up). *It'll be okay. You're fine. There's nothing to be afraid of.*

But I was afraid. More and more, I could feel the not-me peeking out. I would stop crying and suddenly start laughing. I'd be panicked and in the next moment cold and emotionless. I'd have vivid visions of my own death and sometimes even plotted it out, but in my fantasy my boyfriend would stop me. No good. He would have to die, too. Both of us together. The only escape.

These thoughts couldn't possibly be mine. I loved him, and my life, and college was exciting, and no one was going to hurt me again. My mom would occasionally stop by our place unannounced and leave notes, but she couldn't control my life anymore. I was okay. Nothing to be afraid of. Everything was fine.

I told him he should probably start staying up all night if he didn't want to die. Other times I'd try to convince him to die with me. Before the demon did something to him. He would hold me and I would shake and we would both cry on the floor until we fell asleep.

This story doesn't wrap up neatly. I eventually tried psych drugs, went off them, was hospitalized, went back on them, started therapy, stopped everything, started again. I married my boyfriend, we split up, got back together, split up, divorced.

I still wrestle with feelings of being trapped in a nightmare, usually when a close relationship becomes too scary. Only now I have friends and supporters around me who can relate to waking nightmares, and we tell each other about how the ghosts of our younger lives show up to haunt us, how the timelines cross and don't line up, how different inner selves emerge to help us navigate the darkness. We recognize abusive dynamics and the effects of trauma. We connect our big feelings and responses to bigger systems we are forced to survive: classism and heterosexism and patriarchy and so much more. And I wonder, what if I had a community like this when I was young and trying to make sense of my demons?

In many ways, though, I was lucky then. College educated, white, and small, I wasn't perceived as a threat and was able to talk my way out of the psych unit that first time and never go back. I knew enough not to tell anyone in authority about the murderous voices, and I never outwardly hurt myself. Because I "knew" it wasn't real, those I did tell weren't afraid of me.

Am I less "crazy" than someone who doesn't distinguish between the dream and waking life, someone who shouts their truths rather than walls them up inside? Is that why I'm "fine," because I learned to hide?

Trying to Do the Right Things

Malaika Puffer

During the summer when I was fourteen, I went running every day with a stack of Bible verse flashcards in my hands to memorize. "Therefore, I urge you...*pant, pant*...brothers and sisters...*pant, pant*...in view of God's mercy...*pant, pant*...to offer your bodies...*pant, pant*...as a living sacrifice...*pant, pant*...holy and pleasing to God...*pant, pant*...this is your true and proper...*pant, pant*...worship." After so many miles and verses, I climbed up to the top of a large boulder formation to pray before running home again.

I ate meals like a piece of celery, half a can of tuna, and a slice of nonfat American cheese and listened to music like Michael W. Smith. I read the Bible, a low-fat recipe book, and a calorie-counter book. It was all very peaceful and organized for a short while, and I was very much trying to do the right things.

Mom started getting concerned when I did things like bake cookies, refuse to eat them myself, and cry when other people didn't eat enough of them, or when I ate cold green beans from a can for dinner and then just spent some time with an empty fork in my mouth.

Eventually, a doctor asked me if I thought a meal of spaghetti and meatballs and garlic bread with a glass of milk sounded like a normal meal. My impression that that was an impossibly large amount of food earned me a whole team of professionals: a new pediatrician who specialized in eating disorders, a nutritionist, and a therapist.

The rhythm of life changed very suddenly. There was fear buzzing around me, I felt numb and in shock, and my eating habits, which had been very private and almost spiritual, were now a public affair. I was Anorexic, not dieting. And I probably had Depression, they said. When I look back on that time, it was like everything was spinning around me. I had been a well-behaved, high-achieving child, so to suddenly be sick or a problem meant I had to adjust to a new reality. I was put on an antidepressant, and I'm not sure if it was because of that or because of all of the changes, but my energy dropped significantly and I no longer felt any spiritual connection.

There were many battles over eating. There was a time when Mom, Dad, Nana, and Papa all sat around a table, each of them trying different tactics and appeals to get me to eat the plate of food in front of me. I felt guilty for putting them through so much pain because they were obviously upset. One time, my mom and I argued intensely about whether I needed to eat a single raisin that I had omitted. We agreed the single-calorie raisin itself didn't matter. "It doesn't matter, so why should I have to eat it?" "If it doesn't matter, why don't you just eat it!?"

I sought out pro-anorexia communities online and was introduced to a philosophy different from the one I had been raised with. My family and religion taught me that my body was not my own; pro-ana taught me that my body was mine to do with what I wanted. My family and religion taught me that my value was in something external to me; pro-ana and the broader culture taught me I could attain intrinsic value by achieving standards of beauty and performance. I wasn't sure what to believe.

As the summer ended and I entered high school, treatment looked like arguing with my nutritionist about how many calories I needed to eat each day for the upcoming week, only attending school half-time for a while, awkward and pointless therapy conversations, frequent check-ups with the pediatrician, and a steadily evolving medication regimen. I was desperate to be allowed to play sports, so I eventually agreed to eat as much as they wanted me to but started secretly purging. When this was discovered and curtailed, I started hurting myself, which a few other girls in my class were already doing. I thought cutting would be painful and scary, but it was actually easy and exhilarating.

One day I was in my room doing homework when I heard my dad get a phone call downstairs. He then angrily came up the stairs and into my room. "That was the school nurse, and she says someone told her they saw in the locker room that you have been cutting yourself." He yelled at me to drop my pants and lift my shirt so he could see my thighs and stomach. I was afraid and did as he asked.

It was some time after this that I told my pediatrician that something rather benign was "against the rules." She asked about these rules, and I was somewhat surprised by her confusion. The rules...who doesn't know about the rules? "Where did these rules come from?" she wanted to know. "They just dropped into my head," I explained, not thinking it was that strange but not having more of an explanation. No, I didn't think I made them up, they just were there. She seemed concerned and wanted to know much more about this, and whether I was seeing or hearing things. I didn't think I was, but then I became a little concerned because how would I know if I saw or heard the same things as everyone else?

She put me on Geodon, an "antipsychotic," in hopes that it would help with this thinking, which was later described as "rigid with a psychotic flavor," and with eating disorder thinking. Geodon did nothing but make me narcoleptically tired.

I was at my friend Brooke's house one day when I overdosed. Perhaps I had broken a rule and needed to punish myself, or maybe I wanted to feel sick and not be able to eat. I don't know. I wasn't trying to die. I was deeply ashamed when my family, some teachers, and my basketball coach visited me in the pediatric intensive care unit. I was so embarrassed to be there, of the cuts on my arm, and of the smell of sulphur wafting off my body from the medication I was taking to counteract the overdose.

After a while I was transferred to the Brattleboro Retreat. After the whirlwind of arriving, being oriented to the unit, and saying goodbye to my parents, there was a moment when reality sunk in. There were bars on the windows, locks on the doors, white walls, staff monitoring the hallway...this was a psych ward. Crazy and dangerous people get locked up in

psych wards. But I'm here. Am I crazy and dangerous? I must be. I punched the wall.

In the beginning, I hated being at the Retreat. I
didn't need to be there. Other patients helped me adjust to life on the unit. I was scared of them at first,
but I came to really like them. Two kids got in a fight,
and we saw staff restrain them before we were put in
the group room for what felt like a very long time, listening to them scream and struggle. Later, we were
back in the group room, listening while another friend
was forced to get a feeding tube. I was afraid and
learned from this what could happen if you didn't
comply enough. The actual danger seemed to be from
the staff, not from the other allegedly crazy patients.

Because of my negative experience with Geodon, my parents were hesitant about adding new medications. The unit social worker sat us down in a room
with a cartoonish diagram of a brain and explained
that I had a chemical imbalance, so medication was
necessary, like insulin for diabetes. I accepted this, and
I wanted my parents to as well so they wouldn't be
mad or disappointed with me for my actions and feelings.

That first stay at the Retreat was a beginning.
The rest of my adolescence—until I was twenty-
three—was spent in some form of treatment. Some-

times I just did therapy and meds; other times I was in and out of psych wards, in residential programs, or something in between. On my fifteenth birthday, while I was in a residential program in Arizona, I was threatened with being sent to the Arizona State Hospital and told that my parents wouldn't be able to get custody of me again if I didn't stop superficially self-harming. I was made to carry around a garbage bag full of recycling with a sign on it that said "SHAME" until I agreed to share the details of some sexual trauma I experienced as a child.

Coercion like this got me to comply with their immediate demands, but it changed my perception of myself and my role in the world and created much more pain than I already felt. The more that people tried to stop me from hurting myself, even in small ways, the more compelled I felt to jump at any opportunity to do so. I eventually became so focused and intense in my cutting that, at one time, the treatment plan was to place my upper body in a cast as a sort of restraint. When I made a serious suicide attempt in a psych ward, a nurse yelled at me for getting blood on some linens and threw a pillowcase at me. The stories go on and on.

I believed I was sick, and I believed I was a moral failure. I heard both narratives loud and clear.

There was no exploration of how being a girl affected my experience of life and of madness. There was no space to think about the reality or relevance of my sexual orientation. There was no curiosity about the effect of my inherited fundamentalist beliefs. There were just "symptoms" and "behaviors." I was victim and perpetrator, a closed system. No one said I couldn't talk about gender, capitalism, or religious indoctrination, but I wouldn't have known how.

Once, in a residential eating-disorder treatment program, we had a short group about body image in which we looked at beauty standards throughout history. I saw that beauty ideals had changed and weren't universal. We were shown how magazine pictures are edited to make the models look thinner. I was completely enraptured and wished I could learn more things like that every day. There was a context to what we were experiencing.

I have much more context now for all of my experiences than I did as a teenager, and listening to other people's stories of how they made sense of what they went through—all kinds of different ways of making sense—has freed me to find my own meaning. The presence of those rigid rules, which seemed so confusing to my providers, makes sense to me now. There was a lot of uncertainty for me then about what was good, what gave me value, how I should behave, who I was. This uncertainty was the result of entering treatment and the subsequent shift in my identity, the religious and secular worlds I moved between, and being in transition between childhood and adulthood. The arrival of a clear set of rules created clarity, direction, and safety. It was as though part of me was expressing the pressures I felt by providing me with order.

Looking back, I empathize with my parents and providers for their predicament. They must have been terrified. They so clearly saw the risks of what might happen if I were left alone. I might have died. My younger sister had a friend who died of an overdose at thirteen. We heard stories and statistics about deaths from eating disorders. I might have also just continued to suffer—sad, alone, tormented. So they made sure I got into treatment—public treatment, private treatment, secular treatment, religious treatment.

And yet, I did suffer and nearly die. It's not fair to say what would or wouldn't have happened had I not gotten treatment, but I know that a significant part of the suffering I experienced was directly *because* of treatment. Treatment is often thought of as an option that takes away risk, but it also carries its own set of risks. There is no neutral or risk-free option.

How I got out of the mess I was in, and what my life is like now, is too long, nuanced, and precious a story to tuck into a few sentences or paragraphs. The story arc, though, is that the concept of mental illness—the idea that my suffering was primarily about biology, that my thoughts, feelings, and behaviors were not justified or understandable, and that I needed to lower my expectations and dreams for my life— proved to be the source of a lot of my struggle. I know this because, when I undiagnosed myself in a moment that resembled a spiritual conversion, things changed very dramatically.

Life was, and is still, awful and gritty and tragic—but so much more bearable and navigable. I know that psychiatric disability and social barriers exist for plenty of people, regardless of whether they see themselves as mentally ill, and eschewing the disease model is not a panacea. I know my story is not universally generalizable. But it's a true story, so it might be true for others as well.

Much Madness Is Divinest Sense

Jess Stohlmann-Rainey

Much Madness is divinest Sense —
To a discerning Eye —
Much Sense — the starkest Madness —
'Tis the Majority
In this, as all, prevail —
Assent — and you are sane —
Demur — you're straightway dangerous —
And handled with a Chain —

    —Emily Dickinson

I remember when I first learned to hide my madness. I lived in a vibrant world of unreality when I was young, and for quite a while, talking about it didn't differentiate me significantly from other young people. My parents were pretty great at making sure I didn't care, for which I have a deep appreciation in retrospect. One day, while we were playing, my friend said, "You know you're not really Mary, right?"

My world shifted, and I realized I was not like other children. The way I played the roles of figures from our Bibles was fundamentally different from my peers. They were pretending; I was becoming someone else. When my peers traded in their imaginary friends for relationships with each other, I realized that my voices were not the same as their fictional companions. I came to believe there was something wrong with the way I thought, believed...*who I was.*

As it turns out, hiding is profoundly painful. I vacillated between listlessness and unfocused rage as shame coursed through me. I couldn't tell which I hated more, myself or the world, and the rage consumed me. I filled journals with fantasies about being swallowed up by swirling black pits, dying suddenly and tragically. Then the voices that had previously comforted me became more distinct and mean. They perpetually whispered into my ears every terrible thought I had about myself, keeping me awake and distracted for days on end. Eventually, the most malignant began telling me to kill myself—and sometimes other people.

Looking back, my journal entries were prophetic because I was swallowed up. And as I spun violently into the darkness, I swept other people up with me. The only ways I found to bring myself back into my body were painful—booze and drugs and cutting and burning. Eventually I saw one way out and tried to kill myself at school.

Then I began my tour of mental inpatient treatment. After my roommate's suicide in the hospital, I learned that the only way to escape psychiatric clutches was to appear to be the least crazy person in the room. Passing as sane became paramount. When I chose to pass, I distanced myself from the other young people in the ward. I positioned myself as better than them, or at least easier to manage.

Passing is a privilege not all of us mad people are able to achieve, especially if we are otherwise marginalized. It is also a privilege that reinforces the abuses of the mental health system and creates the expectation that mad people should assimilate.

Now I view sane passing as a tactic I might use to advance the movement, not a survival skill. Then, it was the only way I could fathom escaping institutionalization. So I took my pills, complied, and found my way back to the "real world."

The pills wrecked me. I became a neutral, empty shell of who I once was. I was all emptiness and platitudes. The thing that the pills were supposed to be eradicating, my voices, never left me. My family was horrified, but none of us knew what to do.

In my first year of college, I met a group of much older radical ex-patients who taught me to go off my medications by drinking wine. I am certain the wine didn't help much of anything besides making withdrawals less noticeable, but I began to feel free. I developed a relationship with my voices that became helpful and comforting again.

More than anything, I believe activism saved my life. I was liberated by the recognition that the oppressed are not broken or flawed, but living in a world that was never designed with them in mind. I involved myself in radical spaces and was able to feel like I finally belonged.

My connection to sanity is like the tether on a space suit. How close I can pull myself to the ship of consensus reality depends on my amount of concentration and awareness. Any lapse in vigilance and I float away into the comfort and horror of space. The farther away I move, the harder it is to pull myself back or to care about doing so.

Throughout college, I vacillated between pulling myself tightly against the ship and throwing up my hands to float away. I bounced through a number of seventy-two-hour holds, getting the label I am most proud of today: noncompliant. But a label like that comes with consequences.

My final trip to the hospital (I hope), was spurred by my noncompliance. At a protest against ICE, I spit on law enforcement. In the back of the police car, I warned them I would turn the handcuffs to sand and they would be sorry, and I landed in my worst hospitalization yet.

I was put directly into a seclusion room, then pretty quickly put in restraints. An attendant came in and put his hand up under my hospital gown. Once, I wrenched my hip out of the socket trying to escape him, and he unceremoniously popped it back in. He was supposed to be the person who would come in to let me out to go to the bathroom. I would fight him every time, and eventually I bit him on the face and drew blood.

At that point, they added chemical restraints—a cocktail of medications that made it impossible to fight back. I do not know exactly which medications were administered when, but my medical records tell me I was given Haldol, Risperdal, Klonopin, and Valium during my stay. I was there for six days in physical and chemical restraints with a catheter. All I really remember are endless hours of being in a fog, and restraints.

By this time, I had thoroughly learned that traditional mental health treatment was not the path for me. I committed to staying tethered closely enough to reality that I would not end up in restraints again. I invested deeply in informal peer support. The people with whom I found solace are still close to me a decade later. The combination of activism and peer support is magic for me and is the thing I wish for anyone experiencing extreme states to find. We need this kind of network of support because it makes the world safer for us.

This world may not have been built with us in mind, but that does not mean we cannot work to build something better. I have had the opportunity to work in places where I have influenced the mental health system in tangible ways. I am in a leadership position in a crisis center that prioritizes the least-restrictive intervention and has options for both peer support and traditional services. I am part of a state-sanctioned work group to investigate the use of involuntary treatment with people thinking about suicide. All of this has been possible while continuing to experience madness.

I believe the best way we can navigate the world and our extreme states is by loving our madness. Instead of pushing it away, engage with it. To treat it with care and respect, learn whatever it has to teach us. In a world that was built for others, our madness can guide us through the darkest times.

I first read "Much Madness is Divinest Sense" after my suicide attempt in high school. My English teacher gave me a collection of Emily Dickinson's poetry when I returned to school. I didn't fully understand it then, but it kept coming back to me. I had to read it in two different college courses, and it became more meaningful. I lost the poem for years, until recently. I presented about Mad Pride to a class on social justice movements, and afterward the faculty member sent me the poem with a note saying it reminded her of me. When I read it, my breath caught in my throat. It resonated so deeply this time.

What took me years of my life to sort out and countless attempts to articulate, Dickinson captured in just eight lines. What we call madness is a much more reasonable reaction to the world than the way sane people react to madness. Compliance is set up as the only way to prove our sanity, and anything else is met with coercion and restraint. Treating our madness as Divinest Sense, resisting the narrative that compliance and sanity are the same, is the path to liberation.

Contributor bios

The Borderline Academic writes pseudonymously about her experiences as a Mad and disabled person. She hopes to create spaces in which people can express their thoughts and feelings, including romantic obsessions and emotional dependency on others, without fearing judgment or shaming.

Kaz DeWolfe is a digital organizer, blogger, Mad pride and neurodiversity activist, and graphic designer. They are a coordinator of the Hive Mutual Support Network based in Brattleboro, Vermont. Kaz is an editor of *Radical Abolitionist: A Cognitive Liberty Blogspace*. They're a queer, trans, Mad, neurodivergent, frazzled parent just doing their best.

Jodi Girouard is a Vermont writer who tries to use her illness as a tool that allows her to continue to recover with her words.

Jolie Mahan is an artist, organizer, and Mad farmer in Rochester, New York. They study the prison-industrial complex and its connections to ecocide and genocide through settler colonialism and racial capitalism.

Calvin Rey Moen is a queer, trans educator and advocate, a co-founder of the Hive Mutual Support Network, and a former facilitator and organizer with the Icarus Project in New York City. He is also a writer and editor with a regular column in *Counterpoint* newspaper and has published short stories about transgender mutants escaping violence through spontaneous physical adaptation.

Malaika Puffer is a queer, fat woman recovering from psychiatry and evangelicalism in Vermont. She is a co-founder of the Hive Mutual Support Network and a leader of peer support in a community mental health agency, where she advocates for more choice and less coercion.

Jess Stohlmann-Rainey is a researcher, trainer, and advocate who has focused her career on creating pathways to intersectional, justice-based, emotional support for marginalized communities. In her work, Jess centers her lived expertise as an ex-patient, suicide attempt survivor, and person experiencing extreme states.

An Incomplete Resource Guide

This guide can be accessed online at
www.hivemutualsupport.org/MuchMadness.

Many of us have found that doing our own research and sharing books and articles is essential to making sense of our experiences. Trying out new frameworks can give us the language to understand and communicate our own expertise. Showing resources to family members and providers can also be a way of self-advocating and expanding their understanding of extreme states beyond the biomedical model of mental illness. Connecting with peer groups and organizations can aid in self-education and combat isolation, building community and a place to belong.

The following list can be a place to start, which might lead to further discoveries and connections.

Self-Advocacy and Extreme States Webinar

As part of this project, the Hive hosted a panel of speakers who experienced extreme states as teenagers or young adults. Panelists shared their stories of self-advocacy within and outside of the psychiatric system. They shared what in their lives has been most helpful, what hindered or didn't help, what barriers and discrimination they faced, and how they have made meaning of their experiences. Participants joined in a discussion about informed consent and removing barriers to participating in decision making.

A recording of this webinar is available at www.hivemutualsupport.org/MuchMadness.

Groups/Communities

Hearing Voices Network USA
www.hearingvoicesusa.org
"The Hearing Voices Network (HVN) USA is one of over 20 nationally-based networks around the world joined by shared goals and values, incorporating a fundamental belief that there are many ways to understand the experience of hearing voices and other unusual or extreme experiences." Find a Hearing Voices support group, participate in an online forum "for those who hear voices, see visions, or have other unusual or extreme experiences," and find support for providers, family, and friends to broaden their understanding about these experiences.

The Icarus Project
www.theicarusproject.net
"The Icarus Project is a support network and education project by and for people who experience the world in ways that are often diagnosed as mental illness. We advance social justice by fostering mutual aid practices that reconnect healing and collective lib-

eration." TIP offers crisis resources, online peer support spaces, and publications, workshops, and webinars for peers and providers. It operates within a social justice framework that recognizes systemic oppression.

The Hive Mutual Support Network

www.hivemutualsupport.org
www.facebook.com/groups/bratthive

The Hive is an informal, grassroots network based in Brattleboro, Vermont, of people providing each other with direct support and mutual aid in order to decrease reliance on systems that don't or can't meet all of our needs, and which some of us have experienced as harmful or oppressive. The Hive does this through workshops, support groups, a Facebook group, and public events, all of which are intended to help build social networks and, ultimately, to take back the tools we need to navigate living. It is volunteer run, mostly by queer-, trans-, and psych survivor-identified folks.

Advocacy, Respite, and Peer Support Organizations in and Around Vermont

Alyssum

www.alyssum.org

"Alyssum's two bed home is a residential crisis respite and hospital diversion service funded by the

Vermont Department of Mental Health. The program is free to all eligible Vermont residents. It is peer run and designed for people who need short term support while working on recovery and discovery."

Disability Rights Vermont
www.disabilityrightsvt.org
Disability Rights Vermont is a statewide agency dedicated to advancing the rights of people with disabilities and mental health issues. It is part of the National Protection and Advocacy system, which protects people with disabilities against abuse, neglect, and serious rights violations.

Intentional Peer Support
www.intentionalpeersupport.org
"Intentional Peer Support is a way of thinking about and inviting transformative relationships. Practitioners learn to use relationships to see things from new angles, develop greater awareness of personal and relational patterns, and support and challenge each other in trying new things."

Monadnock Peer Support
www.monadnockpsa.org
"As a peer driven organization, it is the mission of Monadnock Area Peer Support Agency (MPS) to promote wellness and recovery, as defined by the individual, through Intentional Peer Support, and to

provide advocacy, educational, vocational, interpersonal, social and spiritual opportunities to adults who utilize mental health services."

Monadnock Peer Respite
www.monadnockpsa.org/peer-respite

"Monadnock Peer Respite (MPR) is for anyone who is experiencing distress and at risk for potential hospitalization due to mental health and feels they would benefit from being in a short-term, 24-hour, peer-to-peer, supported environment with others who have 'been there.' MPR provides a safe place in which each person can find the balance and support needed to turn what is so often referred to as 'crisis' into a learning and growth opportunity."

Pathways Vermont
www.pathwaysvermont.org

"Pathways Vermont transforms the lives of people experiencing mental health and other life challenges by supporting self directed roads to recovery and wellness in an atmosphere of dignity, respect, choice and hope.

"We advocate for the rights of people to live without stigma and discrimination and promote civil rights, community integration, health care, affordable housing and employment for all."

Soteria

www.pathwaysvermont.org/what-we-do/
our-programs/soteria

Soteria is part of Pathways VT. "Soteria is a Therapeutic Community Residence for the prevention of hospitalization for individuals experiencing a distressing extreme state, commonly referred to as psychosis. We believe that psychosis can be a temporary experience that one works through rather than a chronic mental illness that needs to be managed."

Vermont Psychiatric Survivors

www.vermontpsychiatricsurvivors.org

"Vermont Psychiatric Survivors, Inc. is an independent, statewide mutual support and civil rights advocacy organization run by and for psychiatric survivors. Founded in 1983, we offer mutual support, publish a quarterly newspaper that is distributed throughout Vermont, offer patient representation in Vermont psychiatric hospitals and residential facilities, sponsor peer-led support groups, advocate and educate to challenge discrimination, and offer technical assistance to allied organizations."

Western Mass Recovery Learning Community

www.westernmassrlc.org

"The Western Mass Recovery Learning Community (RLC) supports healing and empowerment for our broader communities and people who have been impacted by psychiatric diagnosis, trauma, extreme states, homelessness, problems with substances, and other life-interrupting challenges."

Afiya
www.westernmassrlc.org/afiya

Afiya is part of Western Mass RLC. "Afiya is the first peer-run respite in Massachusetts, and one of only 13 in the country."

Publications

Hearing Voices Network free leaflets and booklets
www.hearing-voices.org/resources/free-downloads

Free publications available for download include:

- "Hearing Voices Coping Strategies," Manchester Hearing Voices Group

"The sheet lists suggestions for coping with the experiences of hearing voices, and seeing visions and having tactile sensations. It is hoped some of these ideas can help you, or someone you care about, towards living positively with these experiences and to maintain a sense of ownership over them."

- *Voices & Visions #1: A straight talking introduction for parents and carers of children and young people who hear voices,* Voice Collective, 2012

  "A pdf booklet aimed at parents/supporters, but also suitable for anyone else who wants to understand a bit more about voices and visions. Includes an overview of the range of experiences people can have, how this can affect them and basic tips on how to speak with your child about them."

- *Voices & Visions #2: A guide to coping and recovery for parents and carers of children and young people who hear voices,* Voice Collective, 2012

  "A pdf booklet aimed at parents/supporters, but also suitable for anyone else who wants to understand more about how young people can learn to cope with difficult voices and visions. Includes a range of strategies, including finding safety, expressing yourself and taking the power back."

- *Understanding Psychosis & Schizophrenia,* British Psychological Society, 2014

  "This booklet presents 'an overview of the current state of knowledge in the field, concluding that psychosis can be understood and treated in the same way as other psychological problems such as anxiety or shyness.'"

- *Power Threat Meaning Framework,* Johnstone, L. & Boyle, M. (2018)

"Published by the British Psychological Society, this document is an overview of the PTM framework. Drawing upon a variety of models, practices and philosophical traditions, its aim is to inform and expand existing approaches by offering a fundamentally different perspective on the origins, experience and expression of emotional distress and troubled or troubling behaviour. It is the result of a working group consisting of people with, and without, experience of psychiatric diagnosis."

"Why Nearly Half of Us Hear Voices (and How to Fix It)," William Lee Adams, *Newsweek*
www.newsweek.com/2015/01/23/why-nearly-half-us-hear-voices-and-how-fix-it-299590.html

A favorable profile of HVN and some of its members that includes statistics about the prevalence of hearing voices and connecting the experience to past trauma like abuse and bullying. The article doesn't actually suggest "fixing" voice hearing but rather making meaning and finding community.

Trauma and Madness in Mental Health Services, Noël Hunter (Springer, 2018)
books.google.com/books?id=ZyVhDwAAQBAJ&dq

"How do survivors of child abuse, bullying, chronic oppression and discrimination, and other developmental traumas adapt to such unimaginable situations? It is taken for granted that experiences such as hearing voices, altered states of consciousness, dissociative states, lack of trust, and intense emotions are inherently problematic. But what does the evidence actually show? And how much do we still need to learn? Noël Hunter is a clinical psychologist working in private practice in New York City. Her work focuses on the link between trauma and altered states, human rights, and alternative approaches to healing."

Counterpoint, Vermont Psychiatric Survivors
www.vermontpsychiatricsurvivors.org/newspaper/counterpoint

"*Counterpoint*…prints artistic contributors (poetry, prose, drawings, paintings, photos, etc.) along with opinions (personal reflections, letters, columns) and news (reports on what's happening regarding mental health issues around the state)."

Clinical research

If you are a student or in higher education, here are some Mad studies and critical psychiatry researchers and articles that might be of interest.

David Cohen
www.madinamerica.com/author/dcohen
Jacqui Dillon www.jacquidillon.org

Akiko Hart akikohart.com
Nev Jones
Joanna Moncrieff
www.madinamerica.com/author/jmoncrieff

Sarah Bögle & Zoë Boden (2019) 'It was like a lightning bolt hitting my world': Feeling shattered in a first crisis in psychosis, *Qualitative Research in Psychology*, DOI: 10.1080/14780887.2019.1631418
(A review of this article can be found at Mad in America: www.madinamerica.com/2019/08/like-experience-first-crisis-psychosis.)

Nev Jones, Casadi "Khaki" Marino & Marie C. Hansen (2016) The Hearing Voices Movement in the United States: Findings from a national survey of group facilitators, *Psychosis*, 8:2, 106-117, DOI: 10.1080/17522439.2015.1105282

Jones, N, Godzikovskaya, J, Zhao, Z, Vasquez, A, Gilbert, A, Davidson, L. (2019) Intersecting disadvantage: Unpacking poor outcomes within early intervention in psychosis services, *Early Intervention in Psychiatry*, 13: 488-494, DOI: 10.1111/eip.12508

Nev Jones & Mona Shattell (2014) Beyond Easy Answers: Facing the Entanglements of Violence and Psychosis, *Issues in Mental Health Nursing*, 35:10, 809-811, DOI: 10.3109/01612840.2013.856971

Schrader, S., Jones, N., & Shattell, M. (2013) Mad pride: Reflections on sociopolitical identity and mental diversity in the context of culturally competent psychiatric care, *Issues in Mental Health Nursing*, 34(1), 62-64, DOI: 10.3109/01612840.2012.740769

Jacqui Dillon & Gail A. Hornstein (2013) Hearing voices peer support groups: a powerful alternative for people in distress, *Psychosis*, 5:3, 286-295, DOI: 10.1080/17522439.2013.843020

Woods, A., Hart, A. & Spandler, H. (2019) The Recovery Narrative: Politics and Possibilities of a Genre, *Culture, Medicine, and Psychiatry*, DOI: 10.1007/s11013-019-09623-y

Moncrieff, J., Cohen, D. & Porter, S. (2013) The psychoactive effects of psychiatric medications: the elephant in the room, *Journal of Psychoactive Drugs*, 45, 409-415
www.ncbi.nlm.nih.gov/pmc/articles/PMC4118946